Introducción a los padres

We Both Read es la primera serie de libros diseñada para invitar a padres e hijos a compartir la lectura de un cuento, por turnos y en voz alta. Esta "lectura compartida"—que se ha desarrollado en conjunto con especialistas en primeras lecturas—invita a los padres a leer los textos más complejos en la página de la izquierda. Luego, les toca a los niños leer las páginas de la derecha, que contienen textos más sencillos, escritos específicamente para primeros lectores.

Leer en voz alta es una de las actividades más importantes que los padres comparten con sus hijos para ayudarlos a desarrollar la lectura. Sin embargo, We Both Read no es solo leerle *a* un niño, sino que les permite a los padres leer *con* el niño. We Both Read es más poderoso y efectivo porque combina dos elementos claves del aprendizaje: "demostración" (el padre lee) y "aplicación" (el niño lee). El resultado no es solo que el niño aprende a leer más rápido, ¡sino que ambos disfrutan y se enriquecen con esta experiencia!

Sería más útil si usted lee el libro completo y en voz alta la primera vez, y luego invita a su niño a participar en una segunda lectura. En algunos libros, las palabras más difíciles se presentan por primera vez en **negritas** en el texto del padre. Señalar o hablar sobre estas palabras ayudará a su niño a familiarizarse con ellas y a ampliar su vocabulario. También notará que el ícono "lee el padre" 👥 precede el texto del padre y el ícono "lee el niño" 👥 precede el texto del niño.

Lo invitamos a compartir y a relacionarse con su niño mientras leen el libro juntos. Si su hijo tiene dificultad, usted puede mencionar algunas cosas que lo ayuden. "Decir cada sonido" es bueno, pero puede que esto no funcione con todas las palabras. Los niños pueden hallar pistas en las palabras del cuento, en el contexto de las oraciones e incluso en las imágenes. Algunos cuentos incluyen patrones y rimas que los ayudarán. También le podría ser útil a su niño tocar las palabras con su dedo mientras lee, para conectar mejor el sonido de la voz con la palabra impresa.

¡Al compartir los libros de We Both Read, usted y su hijo vivirán juntos la fascinante aventura de la lectura! Es una manera divertida y fácil de animar y ayudar a su niño a leer—¡y una maravillosa manera de preparar a su niño para disfrutar de la lectura durante toda su vida!

Parent's Introduction

We Both Read is the first series of books designed to invite parents and children to share the reading of a story by taking turns reading aloud. This "shared reading" innovation, which was developed with reading education specialists, invites parents to read the more complex text and story line on the left-hand pages. Then, children can be encouraged to read the right-hand pages, which feature text written for a specific early reading level.

Reading aloud is one of the most important activities parents can share with their child to assist them in their reading development. However, We Both Read goes beyond reading *to* a child and allows parents to share the reading *with* a child. We Both Read is so powerful and effective because it combines two key elements in learning: "modeling" (the parent reads) and "doing" (the child reads). The result is not only faster reading development for the child, but a much more enjoyable and enriching experience for both!

You may find it helpful to read the entire book aloud yourself the first time, then invite your child to participate in the second reading. In some books, a few more difficult words will first be introduced in the parent's text, distinguished with bold lettering. Pointing out, and even discussing, these words will help familiarize your child with them and help to build your child's vocabulary. Also, note that a "talking parent" icon ⌣ precedes the parent's text, and a "talking child" icon ⌣ precedes the child's text.

We encourage you to share and interact with your child as you read the book together. If your child is having difficulty, you might want to mention a few things to help him. "Sounding out" is good, but it will not work with all words. Children can pick up clues about the words they are reading from the story, the context of the sentence, or even the pictures. Some stories have rhyming patterns that might help. It might also help them to touch the words with their finger as they read, to better connect the voice sound and the printed word.

Sharing the We Both Read books together will engage you and your child in an interactive adventure in reading! It is a fun and easy way to encourage and help your child to read—and a wonderful way to start them off on a lifetime of reading enjoyment!

Habitats of the World / Hábitats del mundo
A Bilingual We Both Read Book
Level 1

---

*With special thanks to Brooke Wagner, Ph.D.
for her review of the information in this book*

Use of photographs provided by Getty Images, iStock, and Dreamstime.
Text Copyright © 2017 by Sindy McKay
All rights reserved

Translation Services by Cambridge BrickHouse, Inc.
Bilingual adaptation © 2017 by Treasure Bay, Inc.

We Both Read® is a trademark of Treasure Bay, Inc.

Published by
Treasure Bay, Inc.
P. O. Box 119
Novato, CA 94948 USA

Printed in Malaysia

Library of Congress Control Number: 2016945519

Paperback ISBN: 978-1-60115-086-8

We Both Read® Books
Patent No. 5,957,693

Visit us online at:
www.webothread.com

PR-11-16

Habitats of the World
Hábitats del mundo

By Sindy McKay

Translated by Yanitzia Canetti

We live on an amazing planet called **Earth**. It is the only planet in our solar system that has liquid **water** and oxygen to breathe. So far, it is the only planet we know of where **life** is possible.

*Vivimos en un planeta maravilloso llamado **Tierra**. Es el único planeta de nuestro sistema solar que tiene **agua** líquida y oxígeno para respirar. Hasta el momento, es el único planeta que conocemos donde es posible la **vida**.*

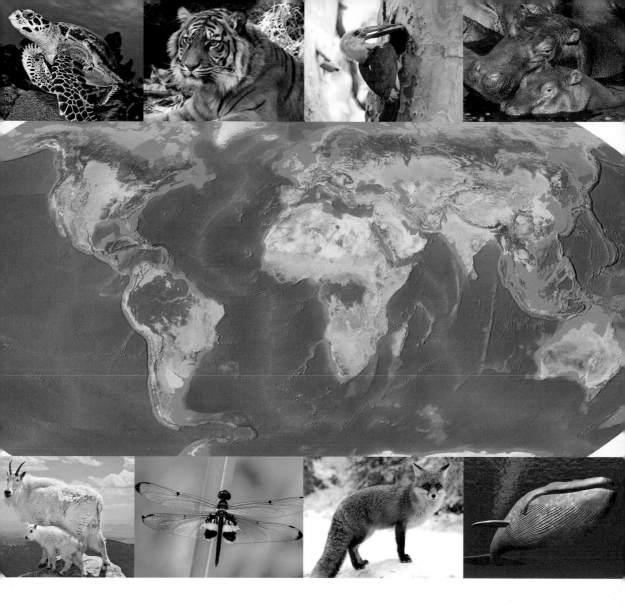

This is a map of **Earth**.
There is **life** on land
and in the **water**.

*Este es el mapa de la **Tierra**.
Hay **vida** en la tierra
y en el **agua**.*

Polar bears • Osos polares

Macaws • Guacamayos

Alpaca • Alpaca

Earth has a huge variety of environments where animals can live. The place where an animal lives is called its **habitat**. A **habitat** provides the right water, food, and shelter for its native wildlife.

*La Tierra tiene una gran variedad de entornos donde los animales pueden vivir. El lugar donde un animal vive se llama su **hábitat**. Un **hábitat** proporciona el agua, los alimentos y el refugio necesario para la vida silvestre del lugar.*

Some **habitats** are cold. Some are hot.
Some habitats have a lot of water.
Some do not.

*Algunos **hábitats** son fríos. Algunos son calientes.*
Algunos hábitats tienen mucha agua.
Algunos no tienen.

The largest habitat on Earth is the **ocean**. The salty water of Earth's five **oceans** covers almost three-quarters of the planet. Just like on land, under the water are volcanoes, mountains, valleys, and plains. Many different kinds of sea **animals** live in this huge habitat.

*El hábitat más grande de la Tierra es el **océano**. El agua salada de los cinco **océanos** de la Tierra cubre casi las tres cuartas partes del planeta. Al igual que en la tierra, bajo el agua hay volcanes, montañas, valles y llanuras. Muchas clases diferentes de **animales** marinos viven en este enorme hábitat.*

Humpback whale
Ballena jorobada

Copperband butterfly fish
Pez mariposa de nariz alargada

Goatfishes
Salmonetes

Sea nettle jellyfish
Medusas ortiga de mar

Some **animals** in the **ocean** are big.
Some are not. A lot are fish,
but some are not.

*Algunos **animales** del **océano** son grandes.*
Algunos no lo son. Muchos son peces,
pero algunos no lo son.

Coral reefs provide a habitat near the shore, where the water is shallow and warm. The reefs sustain over a thousand types of colorful fish as well as dolphins, turtles, sharks, and rays. There are many different kinds of **corals**, and they are all living organisms that can grow and change.

*Los arrecifes de **coral** brindan un hábitat cerca de la orilla donde el agua es cálida y poco profunda. Los arrecifes sustentan más de mil tipos de peces multicolores, así como delfines, tortugas, tiburones y rayas. Hay muchas clases diferentes de **corales**, y todos ellos son organismos vivos que pueden crecer y cambiar.*

Stony corals
Corales pétreos

Green sea turtle
Tortuga marina verde

Acroporidae stony coral
Corales pétreos Acroporidae

8

Soft corals and
Caribbean reef shark

*Corales blandos y
tiburón de arrecife del Caribe*

Various corals and
purple tube sponge in
foreground

*Varios corales y
esponjas de tubo de
color púrpura en
primer plano*

Corals may look like plants, but they are animals.

*Los **corales** pueden parecerse a las plantas, pero son animales.*

Ocean water is salty. The rest of the water on Earth is called freshwater. Lakes are one kind of freshwater habitat. Many plants and animals, as well as many people, depend on the salt-free water of lakes to **live**.

*El agua del mar es salada. El resto del agua en la Tierra se llama agua dulce. Los lagos son un tipo de hábitat de agua dulce. Muchas plantas y animales, así como muchas personas, dependen del agua sin sal de los lagos para **vivir**.*

Rainbow trout • *Trucha arcoíris*

Some animals **live** in the lake. Some animals live on the banks.

*Algunos animales **viven** en el lago.*
Algunos animales viven en las orillas.

River otters • *Nutrias de río*

11

Rivers provide another kind of freshwater habitat. Some animals live in or near the **river**, while others only go there to drink and cool themselves.

Los **ríos** proporcionan otro tipo de hábitat de agua dulce. Algunos animales viven en el **río** o cerca de él, mientras que otros solo van allí para beber y refrescarse.

Hippopotamuses (hippos) • *Hipopótamos*

Grizzly bear • Oso pardo

Bears get fish from the **river**.
Lions drink from the river.

*Los osos atrapan peces del **río**.*
Los leones beben agua del río.

Lioness and cubs
Leona con sus cachorros

Wetlands, such as swamps and marshes and bogs, are habitats where shallow water covers the soil for a good part of the year. It is home to a variety of fish, reptiles, amphibians, mammals, insects, and **birds**.

*Los **humedales**, como pantanos, marismas y ciénagas, son hábitats donde el agua poco profunda cubre el suelo durante gran parte del año. Es el hogar de una gran variedad de peces, reptiles, anfibios, mamíferos, insectos y **aves**.*

Some **wetland birds** eat fish. Some wetland birds eat bugs. Some wetland birds eat fish *and* bugs!

*Algunas **aves** de **humedales** se alimentan de peces. Algunas aves de humedales comen insectos. ¡Y algunas se alimentan de peces e insectos!*

Manatees • Manatíes

Mangrove tree
roots and fish
Raíces de mangle
y peces

⊘ **Swamps** have many trees growing in and around them. A mangrove **swamp** is especially rich in its variety of life. Mangrove trees have enormous roots that provide shelter for fish, birds, turtles, lizards, manatees, and alligators.

*En los **pantanos** y sus alrededores crecen muchos árboles. El manglar de **pantano** es especialmente rico en su variedad de vida. Los árboles de mangle tienen enormes raíces que brindan refugio a peces, aves, tortugas, lagartos, manatíes y caimanes.*

American alligator • Caimán americano

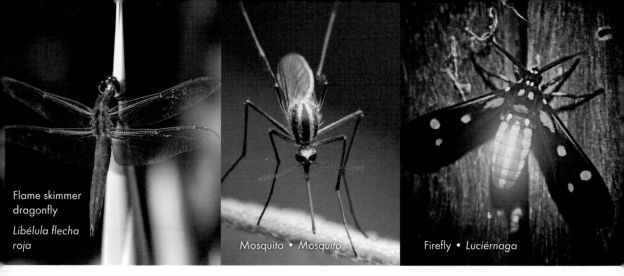

Flame skimmer dragonfly
Libélula flecha roja

Mosquito • *Mosquito*

Firefly • *Luciérnaga*

There are lots of bugs and frogs in a **swamp**. The frogs eat the bugs.

Hay un montón de insectos y ranas en un **pantano**. *Las ranas se comen a los insectos.*

Green tree frog • *Rana verde de los árboles*

Polar bears • Osos polares

The polar regions are the coldest places on Earth. Much of the water is frozen in ice sheets and glaciers. Animals here have a thick layer of fat to keep them warm.

Las regiones polares son los lugares más fríos de la Tierra. Gran parte del agua está congelada en capas de hielo y glaciares. Los animales aquí tienen una gruesa capa de grasa para mantenerse calentitos.

Antarctic fur seals • *Focas peludas antárticas*

Harp seal pup

Foca arpa bebé

18

Chinstrap penguins • *Pingüinos barbiquejos*

There are no plants on the ice,
so lots of the animals here eat fish.

*No hay plantas en el hielo, asi que
muchos animales aquí comen peces.*

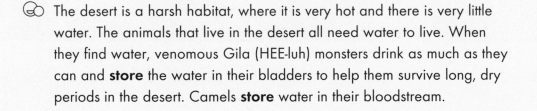

The desert is a harsh habitat, where it is very hot and there is very little water. The animals that live in the desert all need water to live. When they find water, venomous Gila (HEE-luh) monsters drink as much as they can and **store** the water in their bladders to help them survive long, dry periods in the desert. Camels **store** water in their bloodstream.

*El desierto es un hábitat duro, donde hace mucho calor y hay muy poca agua. Todos los animales que viven en el desierto necesitan agua para vivir. Cuando los monstruos de Gila venenosos encuentran el agua, beben tanta como pueden y la **almacenan** en sus vejigas para sobrevivir en los largos períodos secos del desierto. Los camellos **almacenan** agua en su sangre.*

Gila monster • *Monstruo de Gila*

Desert tortoise • *Tortuga del desierto*

Camels do not **store** water in their humps. The hump has a lot of fat. The fat is a way for camels to store food.

*Los camellos no **almacenan** agua en sus jorobas. La joroba tiene una gran cantidad de grasa. La grasa es una forma que tienen los camellos de almacenar alimentos.*

Dromedary camel • Camello dromedario

High mountain ranges are found all around the world. Native plants and animals must tolerate lower oxygen levels and extreme changes in temperature. The animals also must be good climbers! **Goats**, deer, and llamas have hooves especially designed for climbing.

*En todo el mundo existen altas cordilleras montañosas. En ellas, las plantas y los animales nativos deben tolerar bajos niveles de oxígeno y cambios extremos de temperatura. Los animales también tienen que ser buenos escaladores! Las **cabras**, los ciervos y las llamas tienen cascos especialmente diseñados para escalar.*

Moose • Alce

Mountain goats • Cabras montesas

These **goats** have two big toes. Under the toes are soft pads. The pads help them to grip rocks.

*Estas **cabras** tienen dos dedos gordos. Bajo los dedos tienen unas almohadillas suaves. Las almohadillas las ayudan a agarrarse a las rocas.*

Cave • *Cueva*

 While some animals live on mountains, others live inside them. Mountain **caves** provide a perfect habitat for many amphibians, spiders, insects, and some types of fish. Mammals, such as raccoons and bears, may use **caves** to **sleep** in or for shelter in harsh weather.

*Mientras que algunos animales viven encima de las montañas, otros viven dentro de ellas. Las **cuevas** de las montañas proporcionan un hábitat ideal para muchos anfibios, arañas, insectos y algunos tipos de peces. Algunos mamíferos, como los mapaches y los osos, pueden usar las **cuevas** para **dormir** o refugiarse durante el mal tiempo.*

Greater horseshoe bats • *Murciélagos grandes de herradura*

⊙ **Caves** make good homes for bats. They like to **sleep** in caves.

*Las **cuevas** son buenos hogares para los murciélagos. A ellos les gusta **dormir** en las cuevas.*

Persian trident bat • *Murciélago del tridente persa*

White-tailed deer
Venado de cola blanca

Deciduous (dih-SIJ-you-us) forests are especially beautiful in the fall before the trees lose their leaves. Some animals, such as deer and elk, live in this habitat all year long. Other animals, such as birds and butterflies, migrate to warmer climates when the weather turns cold. Bears stay in the forest and **hibernate**.

*Los bosques de hojas no perennes son especialmente hermosos en el otoño antes de que los árboles pierden sus hojas. Algunos animales, como los ciervos y los alces, viven en este hábitat durante todo el año. Otros animales, como las aves y las mariposas, migran a climas más cálidos cuando llega el invierno. Los osos permanecen en el bosque donde **hibernan**.*

Grizzly bear and cub
Oso gris con su cachorro

Bears do not eat or drink
when they **hibernate**.
They wake up in the spring.

*Los osos no comen ni beben
cuando **hibernan**. Se despiertan
en la primavera.*

Coniferous forest • *Bosque de coníferas*

Barred owl • *cárabo*

Lynx • *Lince*

◎ A coniferous **forest** contains mostly evergreen trees, such as pine and fir. In this habitat, the winters are long and the summers are cool. Large predators, such as bears, lynx, and wolves, can be found here. Many plant eaters also make this their home.

*Un **bosque** de coníferas tiene muchos árboles de hojas perennes, como pinos y abetos. En este hábitat, los inviernos son largos y los veranos son frescos. Aquí se pueden encontrar grandes depredadores, como osos, linces y lobos. También es el hogar de muchos comedores de plantas.*

Deer, elk, and moose eat the plants in the **forest**. The plants are on land and in the water.

*Los ciervos, los antes y los alces se alimentan de las plantas del **bosque**. Las plantas están en la tierra y en el agua.*

29

Tropical rainforests sustain more than half of all species of plants and animals on Earth. Rainforests contain four **layers** of habitat—emergent, **canopy**, understory, and floor. The emergent **layer** gets the most sun. Living here are **monkeys**, birds, butterflies, **lizards**, and bugs.

*Las selvas tropicales sostienen más de la mitad de todas las especies de plantas y animales de la Tierra. Las selvas tropicales contienen cuatro **capas** de hábitat: emergente, **dosel**, sotobosque y suelo. La **capa** emergente es la que más sol recibe. Aquí viven los **monos**, las aves, las mariposas, los **lagartos** y los insectos.*

Sun conure parrots
Cotorritas de sol o periquitos dorados

Three-toed sloth
Perezoso de tres dedos

Parson's chameleon
Camaleón de Parson

Lots of animals live in the **canopy layer.** Birds, **monkeys**, and **lizards** are just some of them.

Un montón de animales viven en la **capa** de **dosel**. Las aves, los **monos** y los **lagartos** son solo algunos de ellos.

Spider monkey
Mono araña

Keel-billed toucan
Tucán piquiverde

31

The understory layer is the area beneath the leaves of the trees. It is made up of vines and other dense vegetation. Here you find more birds, butterflies, snakes, and frogs. Beneath the understory is the **forest floor.**

*La capa de sotobosque es el área debajo de las hojas de los árboles. Se compone de vides y otra vegetación densa. Aquí puedes encontrar más aves, mariposas, serpientes y ranas. Debajo del sotobosque está el **suelo del bosque**.*

Giraffe beetle

Escarabajo jirafa

Blue Morpho butterflies

Mariposas morfo azul

Strawberry poison dart frog
Rana venenosa flecha roja

Bengal tiger
Tigre de bengala

Indian elephants
Elefantes indios

Mountain gorillas
Gorilas monteses

The **forest floor** gets little sun. Here you will see tigers, gorillas, and elephants.

*El **suelo del bosque** recibe poco sol. Aquí podrás ver tigres, gorilas y elefantes.*

Grasslands provide a completely different habitat for animals, with open areas of grass and other low-growing plants. There are few trees or places to hide, so speed is important for the animals here. The grasslands of North America are called **prairies**.

*Los pastizales proporcionan un hábitat completamente diferente para los animales, con áreas abiertas de hierba y otras plantas de poco tamaño. En ellas hay pocos árboles o lugares para esconderse, por lo que la velocidad aquí es importante para los animales. Los pastizales de América del Norte se llaman **praderas**.*

American bison (buffalo) • *Bisonte americano (búfalo)*

Black-tailed prairie dogs • *Perrito de la pradera de cola negra*

Skunks and **prairie** dogs live here.
Prairie dogs are not dogs.
But they do bark!

Las mofetas y los perritos de la **pradera**
viven aquí. Los perritos de la pradera
no son perros. ¡Pero sí ladran!

Giraffes • *Jirafas*

African grasslands are called **savannas**. Elephants, rhinos, and giraffes munch on the trees and grasses here. **Lions**, cheetahs, and hyenas are some of the predators on the **savanna.** The predators prey on herds of animals, including giraffes and **zebras.**

*Las praderas africanas se llaman **sabanas**. Los elefantes, los rinocerontes y las jirafas saborean las hojas de los árboles y las hierbas aquí. Los **leones**, los guepardos y las hienas son algunos de los depredadores de la **sabana**. Los rebaños de animales, como jirafas y **cebras**, son presas de los depredadores.*

African elephants • *Elefantes africanos*

White rhinoceros and baby (calf) • *Rinoceronte blanco con su bebé (becerro)*

Animals on the **savanna** run a lot. **Lions** are fast, but **zebras** run faster.

Los animales de la **sabana** *corren mucho. Los* **leones** *son rápidos, pero las* **cebras** *corren más rápido.*

Lions • Leones   Zebras • Cebras   37

Life thrives in the different habitats on our planet. Unfortunately, many of these habitats are in danger. Pollution and cutting down forests can harm or destroy habitats. When this happens, it is hard for animals to **adapt** and survive.

*La vida prospera en los diferentes hábitats de nuestro planeta. Desafortunadamente, muchos de estos hábitats están en peligro. La contaminación y la tala de bosques pueden dañar o destruir los hábitats. Cuando esto sucede, es difícil para los animales **adaptarse** y sobrevivir.*

Black bear • Oso negro

Some animals will **adapt**,
but some will not.

*Algunos animales se **adaptan**,
pero otros no.*

The beauty and diversity of the plants and animals on Earth are truly remarkable. It is our responsibility to preserve and protect this wondrous planet for future generations.

La belleza y la diversidad de las plantas y los animales de la Tierra son verdaderamente extraordinarias. Es nuestra responsabilidad preservar y proteger este maravilloso planeta para las generaciones futuras.

Bottlenose dolphins

Delfines nariz de botella

Red-eyed tree frog

Rana de ojos rojos

Empe
pengu

*Pingüir
emperado*

40

👀 It is up to all of us to take care of the Earth.

El cuidado de la Tierra depende de todos nosotros.

If you liked **Habitats of the World**, here is another
We Both Read® book you are sure to enjoy!

*Si te gustó **Hábitats del mundo**, ¡seguramente disfrutarás
este otro libro de la serie We Both Read®!*

Amazing Eggs / Huevos asombrosos

Enter the fascinating world of eggs and hatchlings! Birds hatch
from eggs, and so do reptiles, amphibians, fish, and insects.
Even dinosaurs came from eggs! Learn about some of the most
amazing animals on the planet and how they begin their
lives—hatching from an egg.

*¡Entra al mundo fascinante de los huevos y los pichones! Las
aves nacen de huevos, al igual que los reptiles, anfibios, peces
e insectos. ¡Incluso los dinosaurios salieron de huevos! Estudia
y aprende acerca de algunos de los animales más impresio-
nantes del planeta y la forma en que comienzan sus vidas: con
la eclosión de un huevo.*

To see all the We Both Read books that are available,
just go online to **www.WeBothRead.com**.

*Para ver todos los libros disponibles de la serie We Both Read,
visita nuestra página web:* **www.TreasureBayBooks.com**.